Mom,

You ... Write for Amazon

Beginning Steps for Beginning Authors

This book was written by a pastor that I have met personally. He gives pointers for writing your book. I have this book on Kindle and have learned many helpful

Ralph Moore

A Straight Street Publication

tips. Let's finish our books this ~~year~~ year! (2023) Love, Alex

ISBN: 1494334844
ISBN-13: 978-1494334840

CONTENTS

WHY YOU SHOULD READ THIS BOOK

The world needs the information rattling around inside your brain.

I enjoy the great privilege of friendship with some very productive people. Many of them confess a desire to write, but never get around to swinging the bat.

The driver for this little book is the fact that there are too many untold stories in the world.

Overcoming Process Intimidation

I'm privileged to travel to every continent in the world and meet many people with great stories. Many tell me that they have the makings of a book inside of them but feel intimidated of the writing process. They seem fearful that they will bog down in the details and never finish a project, so they never start the process.

Intimidation is the *primary* reason why people never get around to writing their life-message. This is where I come in. You can read this short book in a little more than an hour. It is a guaranteed intimidation shrinker!

Beating Fear of Rejection

A *second* reason people don't write is a fear that publishers won't touch their stuff.

Sadly, they may be right on that score. First-time authors face great difficulties with publishers, unless they bring a *large audience* to market.

Publishers are in business to turn a profit. Therefore, money is central to their choice of authors. Their issue often isn't quality, but quantity. You bring a large built-in audience, or a publisher can't afford to work with you.

Now, however, there is a solution for first time authors. It deliberately aims toward small-volume publishing. It is called Amazon.com.

Two Great Venues for You

If you are a first-time author, Amazon built two separate Kindle formats with you in mind. You can publish your book as both an e-book and a paperback.

Both are designed around the person who has great content but only a small audience. The past problem with small-volume publishing is that it was so expensive. The publisher couldn't afford to invest heavily to publish, or to market, a book that might sell fewer than 2,000 copies.

The profits in publishing have traditionally been in high volume retail sales. That all changed with the advent of e-books and something called "print on demand." New technology allows Amazon to make money by printing a single copy of your book. We'll look at that later, but for now I have a few questions for you…

Questions for You…

Do you have a great story, but a limited audience? Is your story worth reading?" Would it benefit even just a few hundred people? If so, keep reading, this book is for you!

Could *you* use a book as an ultra-effective business card?

Just about every candidate for President of the United States begins their campaign by writing a book. In a world of short soundbites, a book gives a person an opportunity to share their life, emotions, vision and values with an audience.

You may benefit from a book which sets forth the vision and values for your organization. I used a book called "Let Go of

The Ring" to introduce the vision of our new church to the people of Hawaii when we arrived from California.

If It's Worth Reading, It's Worth Writing

You may inspire families to hang together rather than suffer the pain of divorce. You may save someone's life. My books on anxiety and stress continue to help people find their way out of the woods. I talk to thousands of people each year, but the books I wrote go to places I never will.

If you have something worth hearing it is worth saying. And, if you could write a book worth reading it is worth publishing.

This short book has three goals: A. To show you what Amazon can do for you. B. To hold your hand while we get your thoughts into a readable format. C. To teach you the ins and outs of Amazon's publishing tools and marketing your stuff.

The kicker is that you can do this without a big audience. Nor do you need to spend any up-front money at a "vanity publisher" where you pay someone to print your book then find yourself left storing inventory under your bed.

Amazon publishing options are waiting for you. Kindle publishing was designed to work with people like you. And they are successful at what they do.

The Pew Research Center published a poll in USA Today which shows that e-books accounted for 20 percent of all book sales last year. The same poll says that sales have increased in the triple digits over each of the past three years.

Forty six percent of people under age 40 own a Kindle or similar e-reader. That number is up from just 18 percent in 2011. Kindle software is free for users of smart phones, tablet computers and other devices. Your world just got a lot bigger.

Brick and mortar bookstores are largely cut out of this equation. I just heard of another large bookseller going under due to the advent of online book sales.

Electronic publishing seems set on conquering the world. Amazon adds the possibility of selling paperback versions of books at very little cost to themselves—this wonderful machine is all set to put your story into print.

Thirteen Things You'll Learn:

1. How Amazon can afford to publish first time authors.
2. Six benefits unique to Amazon.
3. Seven ways in which Amazon will help you sell your book.
4. Why Amazon pays authors nearly five times as much as conventional publishers.
5. Three tools for smashing "writer's block."
6. How to get past the first draft roadblock.
7. Eight ways to hold a reader's interest.
8. A few simple disciplines to make your project much easier and fun to write.
9. How to get by with a little help from your friends.
10. Three simple devices to help sell any book.
11. How to best display your expertise and authority on your chosen subject.
12. Keyword tools designed to help readers discover your book.
13. How to enlist readers as your agents in order to help others find your book.

Read on and we'll discover how easy this is…

SECTION 1:

Amazon Will Make An Author Out of You

CHAPTER ONE

MONEY, MARKETING AND BEGINNING AUTHORS

Electronic publishing works well for authors with a *small* "built-in" audience.

If you regularly interact with a large audience, a traditional publisher wants your email address. But, what's a person with a great message but only a small audience to do?

Ordinary publishers float their boats by churning out books which sell around 2,000 copies. Those are their bread and butter. Unfortunately, the author of such a book often works for something that approximates minimum wage (I know this from experience).

If you have a "built in" audience of around 10,000 people you are eligible to work with a traditional publisher, depending on the quality of your work. If your audience is smaller, Amazon is for you.

I had the good fortune of working with Regal Books for more than a decade. But a couple of my books barely made the cut and I made little money (As did Regal). Recently, my books on disciplemaking and church multiplication were purchased by Baker books. A move that seems a blessing.

The conventional publisher only makes serious money when the *occasional* book breaks into huge numbers. The same could be said of authors.

Money Matters

Conventional publishers and authors are at a disadvantage due to the advent of discount dealers, like—you guessed it, Amazon. When books go for a discount, the author makes *less than* the normal royalty (which is somewhere in the vicinity of 15 percent). When a book gets discounted, the author eats more than their share of the loss. Some of my royalties have fallen to as little as five percent when sold through a discount outlet like Amazon or ChristianBook.com.

If you write for a conventional publisher, Amazon can be your enemy since they discount every book they sell. Not a very promising situation when you consider that you get paid only a small percentage of each sale.

However, if you write *for* Amazon instead of a conventional publisher, you fare better for two reasons. First, Amazon is generous toward authors. They pay a 70 percent royalty on electronic books and about 35 percent on paperback books. Stop and compare those numbers to the 15 percent offered by conventional authors (before the discounters get involved). You get the picture…

The second reason for working with Amazon is that you don't need to present the publisher with a potential audience large enough to buy 2,000 books.

Publishers Buy Audiences, Not Books

Please remember what I am about to say… "Every publisher is *primarily* interested in your audience and only *secondarily* interested in that book which burns in your soul." Publishers sell books, but they buy audiences.

Now don't get all nasty about greedy publishers caring more about money than content. The truth is that they need to make money, or they go out of business in a hurry. Posting a profit is not a bad thing either.

Also, please realize that when you write and publish a book you are selling a product to a buyer. The publisher is the buyer in this equation.

As an author, your customer isn't some guy at an airport bookstand, it is the publisher whom you dearly hope will purchase your book. Only the publisher isn't just buying your book, he's buying your market (I know I already said that, but you didn't believe me, so I said it again).

No publisher can afford to advertise an unknown writer into a best-selling author. This might happen occasionally, but the numbers don't favor the publisher who attempts it.

Unless you are a *very* big shot, the average publisher won't (can't afford to) spend a ton of money on your product.

On the other hand, if you are a politician at the end of your career, a sports figure who just won a championship, or a religious leader who got caught doing something really bad you can expect lots of advertising and promotion from most publishers. They simply hitch-hike off of your reputation and whatever publicity you generated through news media. Remember, this is a business not an art form.

You Do Most of The Marketing

The basic marketing package for most authors looks like this: A) The publisher inserts your book into their catalogue under "New Releases." B) Publishers may arrange a few radio interviews. C) You promote your own book via email, social media and any public speaking you might do. That's it!

Did you notice that in the normal scenario *most* of the marketing is left to you? You not only write for the publisher; you also sell for them.

Of course, this is also true in the Kindle world. But the royalties you receive are nearly five times higher than those of a conventional publisher, and Amazon provides a bunch of tools to help you do market your book. The advantage to this is that everyone makes money even if relatively few books sell in any given month. You'll earn even more when you purchase your paperback at the author's discount then resell it at the retail price.

Beware Self-Publishing

Years ago, I met a famous author (Actually, I've met several, but more about that later).

This guy told me that, as a pastor, I had a built-in audience and that I should self-publish my books.

It worked for him since he spoke to many thousands of people on a daily radio broadcast. He could sell the books by direct mail as well as through bookstores. I had a daily radio broadcast, but it was in a *small* market—self-publishing *couldn't* work for me.

The Problem of Self-Publishing

Self-publishing sounds good, but where are you going to store 5,000 copies of your life's work?

Note that I said 5,000 copies, not 2,000. That's because the cost per copy is *a* little more if you print in larger numbers.

The problems with self-publishing are storage, promotions and the size of your existing market. Also, there is that small problem of the money you need up front to pay for it all. But notice that if you go with a conventional publisher, you'll still be doing most of the advertising, so your real problems come down to that hateful storage issue, the size of your market and up-front costs. By the way, paying a storage center to hold unsold books isn't a profitable idea.

The Dangers of Vanity Press

Then there is what most people call the "vanity press," or "subsidy publishing." This is an entire industry built around would-be authors who pony up a bunch of money to get their book printed. The publisher charges for design, editing and printing your book. The costs can run into tens of thousands of dollars for a couple of thousand books. This is far more than if you simply paid a printer in Hong Kong (Self-publishing). Vanity publishing is self-publishing dressed in a more expensive shirt.

The lure of vanity publishers is their *promise* to market your book. In actuality, they will list it on a website, email a notice to a bunch of bookstores and provide you with a kit so you can promote your own book.

By and large vanity publishing is a rip-off.

Run away from vanity printers. They will lighten your wallet and leave a lot of books collecting dust in your garage. This is because none adequately promotes anything but the "benefits" of working with their company.

What Can A Small-Volume Author Do?

So, we're back to *you* as your strongest source of marketing and advertising. What if we could eliminate *all* up-front costs (Self-publishing and vanity press); do away with storage issues and get you some extra marketing help? Would that work for you?

Turn the page and learn of just some of the tools, which Amazon provides to you as an author. Many seem specifically designed for the first-time author or for someone with a large message but only a small audience.

CHAPTER TWO

HOW YOU CAN BENEFIT FROM AMAZON

There are six obvious benefits to working with Amazon.

Let's skim over them here before getting into more detail in later chapters. My goal is for you to *appreciate* the opportunities in front of your face.

Amazon Owns This Market

We all know Amazon as the world's largest bookstore. They own the e-book market, too. A recent British study found Amazon selling roughly 80 percent of all electronic books. Apple came second with just nine percent.

Amazon currently sells everything from computers to termite bait. But books are where they started. And they now *publish* books as well as selling them. Amazon, the publisher, can help you in a big way.

Amazon Cares About Small Volume Authors

If you have a book in you but possess only a small market the chances are that you'll never write. Or, you may choose between self-publishing and paying big bucks to a vanity publisher. Amazon presents you with a third alternative.

Amazon doesn't need to sell 2,000 copies of your books to make a profit because they do just about everything electronically.

Kindle Books Make Money for Amazon

It's easy to see how they make money off of Kindle books, even if yours only sells a few copies. Amazon's investment is only in the technology that you used to create the book. Everything else is automatic. You interface with a computer as does the buyer. Amazon's Jeff Bezos and company just sit between you collecting profits.

But what about paperback editions of your book? I've found that they are necessary since some people are technophobes and will *never* read an e-book

I first published "Defeating Anxiety" in Kindle, only to have dozens of people ask, "When is it coming out as a paperback?" I returned to Amazon and created the paper version. Actually, that was a dumb move. It would have been easier to start with the print version then moved to format the e-book…but more about that in a later chapter.

"Print on Demand" As A Money-Maker

Technology comes to the rescue of small volume paperback writers as well as authors of e-books.

Amazon's "print on demand" technology gets you and your laptop to do the heavy lifting via their wonderful templates, etc. Afterwards, the computer stores your work on its hard drive and lists it on Amazon's website. A potential reader orders the book. The computer then prints it, including a full-color glossy cover. Finally, a human gets into the act when they package the book for mail.

We're talking about a single copy of your book. Because of *print on demand* technology there are no storage issues or any up-front cash outlay for either you or Amazon. Amazon makes money if they sell a single copy of your book or ten thousand. This is why they can afford to work with you.

Amazon's Templates Make Your Life Easy

After writing and editing your book, you fit your manuscript into one of the easy-to-use, templates ending up with a very nice design for the inside of your book.

The process takes a little time, but you get to review the finished product while working with the tools.

The important thing here is that you needn't pay a graphic artist to design the book (Amazon provides specs so you could hire an artist, but the templates make that unnecessary). With a little trial and error, you will come up with a great product.

After finishing the inside, Kindle takes you through a nice array of cover templates (you supply your own photos) and out pops a beautifully designed print-book.

You can modify the style, color and graphics in their library of templates. You only need to provide photos of yourself and whatever photo you might desire for the front cover of the book. I'll tell you where to get photos when we get around to discussing templates in depth.

Immediately after creating your print, book Amazon will guide you through a fairly simple process, which will render your creation into e-book format.

You will love this process once you get the hang of it.

Amazon Solves Your Storage Problems

Since Amazon stores your book on their hard drive until a buyer orders it, you can keep your car in your garage. I usually order a number of paperback copies of my book for distribution at various speaking engagements but even that inventory is minimal since Amazon delivers so quickly.

There are no storage issues for you and none for Amazon since they never store more than a few gigabytes on a hard drive.

Amazon Works Hard to Promote Your Book

You'll still be the *primary marketing agent* for your book. Your use of social media and direct email come in very handy at this point. But once you get the initial word out, Amazon *steps in* to aid you in several practical ways.

Because it is web-based, Amazon is able to provide numerous tools designed to help you sell your book.

They give you your own "Author Page." They display a "Book Description," which you write yourself. This is a great tool if you take the time to make it work for you. Amazon offers free samples, through either their "Look Inside" feature for both print and e-books. They even offer a prospective buyer the opportunity to download the first 10 percent of your book for free.

You also get the benefit of "Customer Reviews." And finally, there is that handy notification called "Customers Who Bought This Item Also Bought…"

Finally, Amazon allows *you* to give free copies of your book in order to stimulate sales. The program works through something called "KDP Select." When you give the book away, both you and Amazon advertise its availability.

People love freebies. Did you notice that Amazon provides three avenues for people to sample your book for free? There is the free, Look Inside; the free First 10 percent and finally the opportunity for you to distribute the book for free for a couple of days at a time. That's not all...Amazon also gives its "Amazon Prime" members the opportunity to download and read your electronic Kindle book for free as a "borrower." The kicker is that Amazon pays you a couple of bucks for every book borrowed.

Amazon Pays Well

I hope you want to write because you have *something to say*. But, getting paid for it doesn't hurt along the way. Remember, because of their technology, Amazon can pay you nearly *five times* what you would receive from a conventional publisher. And you receive payment whenever someone borrows your book via the Kindle library.

All of this equates to heaven for a beginning or small volume author—take advantage of it.

My own books sell regularly but not in large volume. Yours will probably do the same unless you are wildly successful.

Think of money in these terms—Retired people can generally spend four percent of their investments every year and never run out of money. In that scenario, a $10,000 investment is worth just about $40 per year as spendable cash. If your book sells just five copies each month, you get the equivalent of having an extra $10,000 in your investment portfolio. Hence, even a slow selling book is worth ten grand. Start writing…

CHAPTER THREE

SEVEN WAYS AMAZON HELPS MARKET YOUR BOOK

Remember, publishers are *not* in business to create art.

They *need* to make money if they plan to survive. Amazon is no different from any other publisher in this regard. They must turn a profit to survive.

Amazon invented several tools to help you sell your book, so *they* make more money. For them to make money off your labor, more people must purchase your books. That works for you!

1. Rating the Book Through Social Media

The first Amazon device is a simple request to rate the book at the close of every Kindle Book (Sorry this doesn't occur in print books). The reader gives the book one to five stars and can write a few words about it. Amazon then pops the rating out via the reader's social media platforms. This is a great tool, and even better when used in conjunction with all the others.

2. Give It Away—For Free!

The second Amazon tool helps sell *both* paperback *and* e-books, but you work it through the Kindle dashboard.

You, the author, must first join something called KDP Select (Free) for this to work. If your book is in KDP you agree not to sell it via any other electronic media outlet. Since Amazon just about owns the e-pub market, this is no big deal.

If your book is registered with KDP you can offer it for free on five days out of every 90-day period. You choose the days and you decide if it goes free one day at a time, two days or all five in a single shot.

Giving it for free gets more people liking it, recommending it and doing that little rating thing I mentioned in the paragraph above. This generates momentum.

Though it's a function designed for the Kindle reader, it helps promote paperback sales for people who still like the feel of paper in their hands. Of course, this is a word-of-mouth function. A person has to download, read and enjoy your book before recommending it to a friend who then purchases it either as a paperback or as an e-book.

One great time to give a book for free is right after Christmas. There are millions of new Kindle owners looking for free stuff during the week between Christmas and New Year's Day. Otherwise, give it away on Wednesdays and Thursdays because those are the days when social media gets the most use. You promote your freebie, hoping your friends will share your message about the free book with others.

3. A Daily List of Freebies

All of this gets even better when you discover the third Amazon tool for marketing your baby.

Amazon publishes a daily list of free books. The list is quite long but is searchable by topic.

My wife discovers lots of free books by searching Amazon's front page for "Free Kindle" and then adding a single word, which categorizes the subject that interests her. Because she uses this function quite often, Amazon sends her email notifications of free books that correlate with her previous selections.

I'm not sure about this but it also appears that the list of free books which a reader receives is generated by a computer algorithm which 'knows' the reading habits of that person.

The people who like books like yours will discover that yours is free that day (you tell them about it through social media and email). Hopefully, they will tell their friends and you'll see a measurable increase in sales.

One caveat here is to remind yourself that the freebies aren't lost sales but an increase in the number of people "selling" your book. I was shocked the first time I offered a book for free. In a day, more people downloaded it for free than had purchased it in the prior three months. I wondered if it was an error to give the book to so many people who would now never buy the thing. However, a few days later, I saw the sales numbers increase and was glad I gave it away when I did.

4. Amazon Prime

Amazon's Prime membership works to your advantage in a couple of ways.

That's the deal where a person pays a flat fee for certain privileges. They get free shipping on just about everything. They can download a bunch of free movies from Amazon's TV offerings. And, most important to you, they can borrow your book at no additional cost to them.

So, why would *you* want someone to borrow your book at no cost to them? It's simple—Amazon knows that if they borrow it, they will recommend it and both you and Amazon will get more money. They "loan" the book to generate sales. As I mentioned before, Amazon pays you a stipend every time a Prime member borrows your book. So, you have nothing to lose.

There is an additional side to the book borrower that plays into your hands.

A person can only borrow one book at a time. This limitation stimulates sales. As a

Prime member, I'll borrow a book then find myself too busy to read it. Later I discover another book, which I want to borrow. Since Amazon requires that I "return" the first book in order to borrow the second I often *purchase* the first book so I can read it at a later date. Of course, whether borrowed or purchased, if I enjoy a book, I recommend it to my friends. The free loaners are a powerful sales tool.

5. Your Own Amazon Author Page

Did you ever enjoy a book only to wish you had some way to discover a little more about the author?

Amazon's answer to that desire is a mini webpage where you tell your readers a little bit about yourself. Doing so can help create an *emotional* bond with your readers.

You can also add short descriptions of any other books you wrote, whether published by Amazon or by some other publisher. It is free, so be sure to use it.

6. Selling Overseas

Amazon operates as separate entities in twelve countries (as of this writing). They are still expanding so the number of outlets will increase over time.

Each is named "Amazon." For instance, there is Amazon.de in Germany and Amazon.fr (France). But even those companies cross borders, especially with Kindle e-books.

A few weeks ago, I was in Budapest where I met someone living in Russia who had bought one of my books from Amazon in Germany.

A recent trip to Beijing told the story of just about everyone in the room purchasing Kindle e-books from Amazon.jp (Japan). A few weeks later Amazon opened in China, too. The world is getting smaller by the minute.

Amazon doesn't translate books so your books will appear in your native language, no matter which country sells them. Since much of the world can read English, I find that globalization works well for people who write in English.

When I teach in another country, I always take time to introduce my books and tell people how to purchase them in their own part of the world. Beats carrying around suitcases full of books.

7. Amazon Book Reviews

Finally, there is the book review at the bottom of the page where the reader purchased your book. This is an extremely *powerful* tool.

People want to know what others think before spending their money. The fun thing is that lots of readers like to see their own words in print, so they are usually willing to write a short review of the book.

If someone messages me that the book helped them, I always ask them to go back to the page where they bought the book and repeat what they told me. Some do, some don't. Those that do help someone else discover a useful tool that might better their life.

Amazon positioned their company to help you. Every publisher does that to the best of their ability. But most conventional publishers are limited by what they *cannot* do.

Because of Amazon's early and heavy investment in technology, they can do things for you that would be impossible for a conventional publisher. Their strong web presence is actually beginning to drive other publishers out of business.

Remember, Amazon is in business to make money.

They only earn a profit on your book if it sells. As a company, they array themselves to sell books, including yours.

Instead of feeling bad that no conventional publisher is interested in publishing your work, you can partner with the world's largest bookseller. This makes your thoughts available to those who would benefit from them. If you sell to only a few hundred people or if you sell to tens of thousands, the world is a potentially better place. Who would refuse that partnership?

CHAPTER FOUR

PRICING AND OTHER MONEY MATTERS

I hope to have a *message* burning in your heart. I also hope you get paid for it.

My message is my primary motive for writing. However, I'm not opposed to profiting from my labor—the worker is worthy of their hire.

If you write only to make money, you should probably confine yourself to writing fiction. But helping better other people's lives while earning a few bucks never hurt anyone.

By the way, I am not opposed to fiction. I read more of it than anything else. However, the primary focus of this book is for people who feel frustrated that they have a message but lack an opportunity to deliver it.

Most of what I've written in this book is as useful to a fiction author as to those interested in publishing non-fiction. It's just that my focus leans toward the writer of non-fiction.

Kindle's E-book Royalty Window

Let's talk about Kindle royalties for a few minutes.

There is a "window" in which your royalties *double* what you might otherwise receive. Step outside the window and your royalty drops in *half*.

If you price an electronic Kindle book between $2.99 and $9.99 Amazon pays you 70 percent of the sale. Below $2.99 and above $9.99 the royalty drops to "just" 35 percent.

Now compare those numbers to the 15 percent offered by conventional publishers and Amazon just got a lot more interesting. Please remember that conventional publishers aren't ripping people off. They carry overhead that Amazon does not.

Here is an example of reality in the world of royalties: One of my conventional books sells for $14.99. That is only *if* someone happens to purchase the book at a retail bookstore. Which seldom happens as most of my books sell on Amazon whether they publish them or not.

At 15 percent, I get roughly $2.25 for the sale. If the book sells through a discount marketer (like Amazon or ChristianBooks.com) the royalty drops drastically. I not only lose to the discount, but the publisher cuts percentage which I receive as a royalty—I lose to both the discounted price and to the reduced royalty rate.

Do I need to remind you that brick and mortar bookstores are going the way of buggy whips? Fewer books sell at full retail price every year. Not good news for someone in my shoes.

Meanwhile a $4.99 e-book nets nearly $3.50. And the e-book is usually (for me) one fourth as long as the book with the conventional publisher (More about book length in another chapter). I get more money for publishing a *short* e-book than I do for writing a much longer one for a conventional publisher. I currently earn more than twice as much from my few Kindle published books as I do from my relationship with an established Christian publisher. And those books with the mainstream publisher are my core life message. Amazon Kindle works well for me!

We won't look at paperback pricing and royalties here. You can do that on your own, once you understand the e-book deal. However, please do understand that paperback books pay roughly 35 percent. Not as nice as the e-books but still more than twice the offer from a conventional publisher.

Pricing Is Largely Up to You

Here's a question for you: "If your royalty gets cut in half above a $9.99 price point, why would you price your book at $12.99?"

Fair question, wouldn't you say?

Yet a quick search around Amazon will show you lots of Kindle e-books priced from $10.99 to $15.99. I can't understand why anyone would want to throw away that fat royalty. Besides the problem of a reduced royalty, books usually sell in larger quantities when the price remains lower.

Whatever you decide, with Amazon the pricing is left up to you.

I researched this pretty well and discovered that fiction books get priced all over the map. Some very good historical fiction goes between 6.99 & 9.99. A beginner should probably stick with that $2.99 figure until the book gains some momentum. You can always raise the price if it sells well.

Look at what others are doing and price accordingly. However, if you are a beginner, remember that you are an unknown quantity. You need momentum.

You might want to set a higher price, on day one, then lower it to $1.99 or even to 99 cents for a week, just to gain momentum. People like discounts. Remember the only way anyone will know that you reduced the price (never for more than a week) is that *you* tell them. Your twitter message should read, "For one week, beginning today, my $X.XX book will sell at an introductory discount price of $Y.YY."

Remember, you are your own marketing department.

Keep non-fiction books short and $4.99 works well as a price point. There is no magic in this number. It is just what most people do at this particular time. A specialty book, like this one, should sell for more.

One very good book, about writing for Amazon, suggested that if you wrote a nice 160-page manuscript you should "massage" it into a *series* of four, or even five separate books.

This works well for three reasons: A) We live in a short attention span world. B) You will make a lot more money selling four books at $4.99 than if you sell one at $9.99, even if you don't count the higher royalties from Amazon. C) If you master Amazon's tools, your books will sell each other. This is particularly true if you link them as a series.

Where You Put the Money Is Important

Where you channel the income from Amazon is crucial, so pay close attention to the next few paragraphs. This advice about where you place the money is *not* a quick note about investing your way to riches. This is about protecting your larger assets.

You must understand *how* Amazon pays out royalties and *why* you need to protect yourself against identity theft and serious loss of your money.

It Is All Protected by A Single Password

Everything you do with Amazon links to your username and password. This includes your publishing efforts. When you publish with Amazon, the company asks you for bank routing information so they can wire royalties directly to your account each month.

This is a great system except for one flaw…

If you lose your password, Amazon sends an email to establish a new one.

Amazon asks for an email address in the username box. If your username is your *everyday* email address you could be in trouble. Anyone who could hack your email account could then use the email address to ask Amazon for your password.

Whoever has your username and password gains then access to your bank account via the Amazon account management page. There are probably hackers who are smart enough to target Amazon authors for this very purpose. Not good!

Avoiding Bad Habits

I developed the (bad) habit of using the same username and password for everything I did on the web.

I had separate usernames and passwords for personal investments and banking but used the same combination for everything else, including Amazon.

When Amazon asked for banking information, I saw no red flags since I already trust them with credit card info. However, one day I got a fright that is worth mentioning…

Someone emailed me a solicitation for something I didn't want to buy. They had my email address, but that is no big deal. The fact that they addressed me by my *password* was a very big deal. They addressed me as "Dear '*My password.*'" They thought my password was my name so no identity theft occurred, but that password floating around could cause all kinds of trouble.

There is a simple two-stage solution to this problem. First, create an email account with a weird name and use it *only* for Amazon transactions. The password should be *equally strange.* The second half of this equation is to open a *new* bank account, which you use only for Amazon. That gives them a place to send your money but maintains a firewall between that small account and the rest of your banking life.

I put $500 into an account at a different institution from where I do my ordinary banking. Amazon wires money to that account on a monthly basis. The relationship between Amazon and that small bank account never causes any worry over identity theft.

There is a side benefit to this preventative action. It's easy to *forget* money as small amounts automatically dribble into a small bank account. You will be pleasantly surprised every few months as you discover growth in that account.

Money Matters, But It Has Its Limitations

I don't write books to make a lot of money. In fact, some of my books have earned less than minimum wage for the time invested.

I see myself as more of a *propagandist* than a proper author. I'll never be famous or rich and I really don't care.

I write because I want to change the world. Therefore, it doesn't matter if I make a lot of money.

When writing about how to solve personal problems such as marriage issues, anxiety or depression my *goal* is to help people live better lives.

When I write books on disciplemaking and church multiplication, I pray for fire in the heart of some young person much like that which got ignited by authors I read several decades ago.

I even pray for the person who might find my books on some dusty shelf long after I've departed the planet.

You see, this is the wonder of a book—imagine a technology that allows you to stockpile your ideas, send them to other continents, even to *another century* where they might explode into action that you'll never hear about. A book can do all of these things.

I hope you think this way about your own writing. Don't do it for the money. However, do be practical about money—the stuff is useful.

Changing the World

Write your heart out but do it with a goal of bending history.

If you have only a small audience, "So what?" You may light fire in one or two of your readers that changes their lives and those of people around them.

Three books (by three separate authors) published way back in the 1960's turned into all the churches we've planted. One of those books achieved popularity, the other two were largely overlooked—but they changed my life while I was still in my early twenties. Those books resulted in more than 1200 churches planted around the globe.

Write to change history and you'll be a happy camper!

Leave Nothing on The Table

The Japanese have a word called, "Mottainai." It doesn't translate directly into English, but I can give you a fair idea of its meaning.

My wife and I recently attended a wedding reception where the hosts had ordered far more (wonderful) food than the crowd could eat. Great food left over from a fine feast was mottainai.

As you look at your life, you don't want to leave behind a fine feast.

You have thoughts and ideas, which could inspire another person to great accomplishment. Your words could rescue someone from suicide. If you confine yourself to speaking, but not writing, your life will end with mottainai.

Don't let anything God gave you go to waste. This book is about writing for Amazon. But Amazon isn't the point. Writing is! Put your words out there where they can shape history in a good way.

Even the fact that I am writing this book to stimulate you to write others is my way of avoiding a personal sense of mottainai.

I want to *leverage* my ability to write as far as is possible. One way to do this is to induce you to publish *your own* world-changing ideas. This is similar to my motive for making disciples who plant churches—it multiplies the efforts of one individual.

Leverage is tremendous. Mottainai is a rotten waste.

SECTION 2:

Writing Needn't Be That Difficult

CHAPTER FIVE

OVERCOMING WRITER'S BLOCK BEFORE IT BEGINS

Many would-be authors never get the first paragraph into the computer.

They encounter "writer's block" before they ever put their thoughts on paper. If that is your problem, this chapter has your name all over it.

The key to overcoming writer's block is pretty simple. Like a thousand-mile journey beginning with the first twelve inches.

Once you establish a goal and start writing, the book will sort of "unwind" itself. But there are some devices to make this easier.

The practice of writing is pretty straightforward. It is mechanical. You work through the steps, then you energize the material by adding your personality to the information you assembled. In the end, you have a finished book.

The development of a book takes time but is not complicated. Yet I know some pretty smart people who fear the process. They won't even *attempt* to write about subjects, which they know very well.

The activity intimidates them. Hence, the world is a poorer place.

One powerful leader had a mountainous influence on my future through a book, which I read *about* him. Eventually we became friends. He influenced me, and many of my friends, in an even stronger way. For years, we've begged, and cajoled, him to commit his shiploads of experience to paper. He never rose to the occasion. He suffers from the ultimate source of writer's block, which is *fear* of the process.

My Own Fear of Writing

As a newlywed, I wasted a great deal of our small "nest-egg" on a mail-order writing course. The material was useful but didn't work for me.

Since it was a correspondence course, it could not offer emotional support. There was no one to encourage, coax or otherwise get me off my caboose and into gear.

When the first lesson arrived, the company *specified* what I was to write…no problem there. I simply did as they told me. However, the second lesson stopped me cold in front of my antique electric typewriter.

They asked for a 1,000-word story about *any subject* I chose. For me that freedom was hangman's noose. They gave me *too much* liberty. I could write within guidelines but take away the structure and I was a dead man. I stared at blank paper for many hours over several days. Finally, I decided that I wasn't cut out to author anything—ever!

Fear of writing so crushed me, that I ditched the course, though I was obligated to continue paying for it for many months.

I was fresh out of ideas and fearful that whatever I wrote would turn out terrible. An empty *and* fearful mind is a dismal swamp.

The sad thing is that I had always felt that I could, and would, one day write the things I was learning as an aid to others.

When I did write that first book, it was not very good and is no longer in print.

The important thing about that first attempt is that I finally produced *something*. Even then, it never would have happened without the encouragement and harassment of a good friend. This guy thought the things I taught in church were worth reading by a wider audience. Without that friend, fear would have kept me hostage my entire life.

Three Steps to Overcome Writer's Block

Writing is a lonely task and fear of rejection is often the only company you keep as you work.

What you need are vehicles to help smooth the process and overcome fear. You need to work from an assumption that your thoughts are worth reading. That assumption grows as you work through the *early* mechanics of any writing project.

The good news is that there are some tools we can use to help get past writer's block. I hasten to remind you that fear will retreat if you view writing as a *mechanical* rather than artistic exercise.

One of the biggest problems we face as beginning writers that we take on too much at one time.

You need to take a horde of short steps toward that long journey which we call a book. Extensive and random notes combined with copious outlines are excellent first steppingstones toward an interesting book.

You can write without wide-ranging notes and a strong outline, but only with *great difficulty*.

"Free association" works for some fiction authors. It invites a migraine if you try it while writing non-fiction. Lack of a detailed outline *induces* writer's block via confusion over what to include and where to situate it. The outline *always* tells you what to write about next.

The idea is to assemble data as a kind of roadmap to guide you through the procedure of authoring a book. This reduces confusion and intimidating fear. Once you pull the map together, writing becomes a simple matter of moving from one stop on the road toward the next.

1. Get Ahead Through Rabid Notetaking

The first intimidation-killer is a mania for taking notes. I use a tool called ToodleDo for this purpose. It is a *hierarchical* note-taking app, which syncs data between my phone and my computer.

The term, "hierarchical," is important here. That function allows me to organize an otherwise random collection of notes into a loose-knit guide.

The guide later morphs into a roadmap during the outlining phase. Offering folders, tasks and notes, Toodledo allows great functionality and freedom to shape and re-shape a collection of thoughts.

For instance, I have a *folder* named, "Books to Write." There are currently 36 potential book projects in this folder. Most are simply ideas leading nowhere, but some will take shape in a future published book.

In that folder I created a *task* called, "Writing for Amazon." Under that task is a space for *notes.* In the notes section I randomly tossed my thoughts about this book. This process went on for nearly a year before I ever began to think about outlining the information.

A side benefit to this is that some of my ideas became worthy of a separate book—at which point I initiated a new "task" to store those ideas.

After exhausting the flow of ideas in the single note, I began the laborious working outline, which engendered a roadmap for the writing phase.

Fiction writers take notes, describing settings, and people—down to their haircut or the way they scowl. They snatch incidents from the news then twist them to fit their plot. Non-fiction writers can do some of the same with real-life situations and solutions. When you do this, be careful to change names, places, gender and age to protect the people whose stories you tell. Any thoughts and experiences relating to the subject belong in your scramble of ideas relating to the book you hope to write.

I enjoy reading. I mostly love fiction and history. Surprisingly, fiction books do provide the occasional idea for a non-fiction writer. But the history books are a treasure house of workable ideas.

I often begin a book about church life with a sort of a parable gleaned from history. For instance, I used the Allied victory in the Second World War as a vehicle for the primary argument in a book called *"How to Multiply Your Church."* The strategy is to change culture by launching a myriad of small churches in a manner parallel to the Allies overwhelming the Nazis by outproducing their factories and farms during the war. The idea, which grew into the structural scaffolding of the book, emerged out of history of an entirely different nature.

Remember, an idea may seem inconsequential at the moment, but you should note it anyway. You never know when it will combine with another in the shape of something meaningful.

2. Life Is Easier with Intensive Outlining

After collecting ideas, I proceed to outline them.

My goal is to "outline my ideas to death." By that, I mean I intend to create an enormously *detailed* outline of what I will write.

Getting to the outline is easy. Since the notes in my phone sync with Toodledo online I am able to print them in their gloriously jumbled format. I then cut them into strips with a pair of scissors. After that I make piles of notes which grow into what I call "chapter bundles." I slide the bundles into paper folders, which are easy to organize as major points for the outline.

Mark your folders with working chapter titles. Each folder is a chapter in the making. Spread them out on your living room floor making it easier to organize them into the basic order in which they will appear in the book. Remember, these are "working titles." You can always change them later.

After the floor exercise, sort through the bundles of paper scraps, creating the rough outline for each chapter. Remember to do this one bundle/folder at a time. Multitasking makes you nuts.

During this stage, it is important that you've formulate an end goal for the book. You should be able to describe it in a 30-second elevator speech *after* assembling the notes into chapters, but *before* you write the outline.

You will inevitably gather *fresh ideas* while assembling the outline, as you will while creating and editing the manuscript. Be sure to fit them into your project. Once the outlining begins, the book becomes a kind of living organism. What you've written paves pathways into *new territory*.

Both the ease of notetaking and the intensity of outlining reduce my *fear* of writing and *confusion* over, "What goes where?"

During this phase, self-criticism is nearly non-existent. You can relax because you know no one but you will ever see your sloppy notes or your evolving outline. You can suspend fear for later when you actually face the task of writing something.

The purpose here is to produce a viable roadmap. When you start the first draft, you will already know, in detail, what you plan to say.

My overly idealistic goal is for an outline to contain one line for *each paragraph* in the finished book. Of course, I never quite reach that goal. However, a 160-180-page book usually first appears as a 60-plus page outline.

However you look at it, you want to create a very detailed outline from your random notes. The goal is to eliminate an oversupply of freedom. You need boundaries in order to generate clear-eyed prose.

Remember, it is far easier to organize your book while it is still in outline form. Attempts to do so later foster confusion.

You don't want to find yourself modifying structure while trying to write. Some of this is inevitable, but time spent on the outline minimizes time spent walking down back alleys to nowhere.

3. Collect Memorable Phrases, Then Make Them Your Own

Besides gathering my own ideas, I collect "cool phrases" which I discover in my normal reading activities.

Fiction writers are great at painting pictures. I love to steal their phrases, hoping to incorporate them into some future project. Whenever you do this, be careful not to plagiarize. In my case, I always modify other people's phrases. I change a thought enough that it becomes my own work and not a direct copy of someone else's genius.

The Internet helps you research the kind of data, which adds strength to your writing. I normally do this during the outlining phase. During the earlier note-taking period, the data comes almost by accident. Research while outlining is much more directive. You know what you need to add strength to your project.

When writing, "Stress Busters," I mined some great information about the effects of caffeine on our physical health, as well as our mental well-being. In that case, "Web M.D." became a great source for the book. During the outlining stage, it grew obvious that this type of information was necessary to the flow of the book. I had gleaned none of it during the note-gathering months. That website became one of the stops on my roadmap to a successful book on stress management.

Earlier in this book, you read about Amazon's amazing share of the e-publishing business. That was something I discovered in USA Today while *editing* this manuscript. I included it because the chapter seemed to demand reinforcement.

These bits of information are readily available on the web. They add weight to your work. You should gather them during either the note-taking phase, or perhaps when you get into editing and realize that you need support for an idea. Whatever you do, don't overlook this fantastic research tool.

Another research tool is Amazon's "Look Inside" feature.

You identify a book containing information about the subject of your book. Then you type in a keyword and Amazon displays the pages in that book relating to the term you searched. You can gather data and even enough bibliographical information to fully credit the book and author for the help they gave you.

When writing books on church growth and multiplication I've gotten so much help from this tool that I felt obligated to purchase a couple of the more useful books. I now own them for future reference, and I feel that the authors gave me so much help that *honor* bound me to purchase their work.

The Demise of Writer's Block

By now you must agree that the process feels mechanical and almost simplistic. Pull together a roadmap leading to an interesting book requires lots of time but little creativity.

Because the progression is so mechanical, there is little room for fear and self-doubt.

The notes and detailed outline deter writer's block. When writing, you may run out of steam due to fatigue, but you should never hit the wall called, "What do I say next?

CHAPTER SIX

WRITE THE FIRST DRAFT...QUICKLY!

Let's talk about putting words on to paper.

Perhaps, I could better phrase that "dumping words into your computer?" Either way, you do best when you get your thoughts down as quickly as possible. Beginning is half-done!

A first draft is always the awkward part of the process.

This is the time when self-doubt has its way with any author. You want those feelings to pass quickly so it makes sense to compose the initial draft as quickly as possible. I've found a tool, which makes this feasible.

I've learned to *dictate* my first draft using a tool called Dragon Naturally Speaking, from Nuance communications. It types while I talk.

However you write your first draft, it makes for poor reading. It's even worse when you use Dragon Naturally Speaking because, "write-speech," is different from, "talk-speech."

The editing process will vastly improve whatever comes out in the first draft so how you get it there doesn't really matter that much. The important thing is to capture your outline in an *editable* manuscript, and to do it *quickly* so you don't lose confidence in the project.

With Dragon Naturally Speaking I first print my outline, then talk my way through it. A first draft soars into my laptop. Doesn't make for good reading but it accomplishes its purpose. I am left with a workable manuscript which I can massage into a reasonable book.

A Wise Purchase

I'll get into editing in the next chapter, so I want to take a little more space to talk about purchasing the software and learning to use it.

There are three different levels of the product. You need the "Home Edition," which is the least expensive. Best to purchase it directly from the Nuance website, (www.nuance.com).

Don't even think about buying it on eBay or from a discount vendor. I know this from *bad* experience.

A few years ago, I purchased a "used" version of the product but couldn't get it to work. It loaded into my computer nicely but wouldn't activate.

I called Nuance to complain. They were very kind but delivered bad news. The copy I bought was a cleverly disguised knock off. Someone had purchased the software then made duplicates which looked like the real thing. They even copied the packaging. Nuance told me that the product activation code had been used several times before. I wasted my money looking for a bargain.

You may think you don't want to invest the money or perhaps you fear the learning curve. You'll regain both time and money, through time saved, with your first project.

The software is highly intuitive, therefore easy to learn.

You begin working with Dragon by reading a few paragraphs, which they provide, into its database. This teaches it the basics of your individual accent, slurred speech, etc. After the short reading, the software asks permission to analyze every document and email on your hard drive so that it can pick up on your writing style.

After that, there is a correction tool, which allows you to correct the software each time it misunderstands you. In other words, it soon learns how you *mispronounce* words so it can spell out your intentions rather than your sloppy pronunciation.

The "misunderstandings" diminish very rapidly. This is technology at its best.

Your Time Has Value

I assure you that if your time has any value, you'll be happy with the purchase.

I typed the first three chapters of this manuscript on an airplane. It took several hours. I'm dictating the rest of the book and calculate that it will take about a third as much the time as I spent just on those first three chapters.

The tool is a hot bargain. Get it today!

Diminishing the Agony Factor

Don't know about you but I experience lots of misgivings when I write. The haunting question is, "Who would want to read this garbage?"

First drafts are unadulterated misery for me.

I suspect that no matter how many books you produce you will still face that dreaded question. The good news is that the evil voice fades as you shift from writing to editing.

Besides, only one person on the planet has the misfortune of reading your choppy, redundant and poorly crafted first draft.

That unfortunate soul is you! The good news is that what you wrote finally resembles a book, no matter how badly written. This is because you can turn garbage into something worthwhile in the editing process.

We'll talk more about editing in a later chapter. The point here is that it is best to get through that first draft as quickly as possible. If you bog down there you won't experience the joy that comes as you refine your thoughts into meaningful help for another person.

CHAPTER SEVEN

EIGHT WAYS TO MAKE A BOOK FUN TO READ

I used to keep a plaque on my desk that read, "Keep it simple stupid!"

Simplicity is the key to good writing. It begins with efficiency. Shoot to write your story in as few pages as possible.

Remember, you are *not* Leo Tolstoy, and you aren't writing "War and Peace." Today's population is used to social media and gathering information from the internet. All of this tends toward a short attention span. Write accordingly.

As a young author, I gathered some straightforward advice about writing. I kept it in a file until I began writing books many years later. Here are several of those tips that still serve me:

1. Shorter Is Better

Write short sentences.

A terse, minimalistic style suits today's readers. News articles employ short sentences and your audience probably reads the news. Short sentences force you to think clearly and speak directly to your audience.

Create short paragraphs.

Again, this has much to do with people's attention span. One way to help your reader into a new chapter is to begin with a one-line paragraph. Chase that with two lines, and then complete the sequence with a three-line paragraph.

After this lead-in, vary your paragraph lengths. This simple device draws a reader's eyes through the main body of material.

Short paragraphs, of varying length, keep a reader involved and make for an interesting visual presentation.

2. Action Words Move Readers

Use active verbs. The "to be" verb form is a killer. Don't say, "He's going *to be* writing a book." Do say something like, "He's busy wringing a masterpiece out of his computer."

Try to avoid adverbs and adjectives.

Good writing demands strong nouns and active verbs. A simple rule of thumb here is to avoid adjectives ending in "ly." The phrase, "a mammoth creation," is stronger than "monstrously big."

Your work feels tight if you concentrate on linking action verbs to colorful nouns. It feels tightest if you disdain adverbs and adjectives.

3. Colorful Language Entertains

Color your language using the thesaurus in your word processor. While editing stay on the lookout for dull sounding words and replace them via the thesaurus. Stick to vigorous, forceful action-oriented words to spin your tale.

I often brighten my work with a book called, "Words That Sell," by Richard Bayan. This tool works best *after* I've edited my work several times. By that time, I've solidified content, but my words may lack emotion. I simply read through Words That Sell with a pack of Post-It Notes. When I spot a juicy phrase, I mark it with a sticky note reminding me where I think it would fit my creation.

Perhaps, "Words That Excite," better describes Bayan's book. The author lists words and phrases that burrow deep into human emotion.

Banyan's book is well worth the outlay. You'll glean more than exciting words from the book. It presents new ways to turn a phrase. Occasionally Banyan will steer you to new horizons by framing a fresh paradigm for your thoughts.

4. Personal Stories Endear You to The Reader

Describe your *own* experiences as you write. You will establish a closer connection with your readers.

People are interested in other people, especially those who offer them help. Stories about overcoming my fears, as a writer, can help you trounce your lack of self-esteem as an author. Personal stories of overpowering stress and anxiety enliven books I wrote on those topics. Your personal story warms your writing.

Intimate stories also bring credibility to the project. You are something of an expert as you write from personal experience. This is especially true if you've enjoyed either great success in your field, or if you've mastered personal problems.

Weave personal experiences into your outline before you write the book. The more stories, the better the book. Later, during the editing phase you'll find yourself waking in the night thinking about a life event that belongs in the book—fit it in.

5. Write in The First and Second Person

I'm on thin ice here. Grammar books and Word's faithful grammar checker hate the use of words like "I" and "me." But I use them anyway.

Don't get me wrong…I go through my work to reduce the use of personal pronouns, but I leave lots of them in. The reason for this is that they are *personal.* Unless you are penning a textbook, you want to connect with your reader.

Conversation demands personal pronouns. You should hope to engage your reader in a personal conversation. So, dump your English teacher for a new girlfriend. Keep your writing personal and you will benefit more readers.

6. Borrow Phrases Without Plagiarizing

The editing phase is time to harvest those cool sounding phrases that you collected. Just remember to modify them or give written credit where it is due.

When writing scholarly stuff, I directly quote and credit others. But when writing "self-help" books I try to stay away from footnotes. My assumption is that readers looking for help just want to get to the solutions I offer. In this scenario, I find it's best to modify phrases and ideas so they become my own.

This is another place where I try to glean new paradigms of thought. Working with someone else's colorful phrase often sheds new light on my subject or the way I present it. Always remain open to expanding your own ideas with the help of someone else's insight.

7. Stay Positive

Be positive. No matter how tragic the tale, try to find a positive way to say it. Notice that it's better to say, "Find a positive way to say it," than to say, "Don't be negative."

No one wants to hear from a person who drags them into an emotional ditch. You may need to address bad stuff but do it in a pleasant manner. Never give in to attacking others and don't display bitterness.

8. Show, Don't Tell!

Show people what you want them to see, don't lecture through your writing. "Once upon a time," defeats, "You must!" any day of the week.

Here are two different ways to present the same information. You decide which is more effective:

Profile A: "When snow skiing you should try to overcome fear because fear prevents any real fun."

Profile B: "The day I finally learned to snow ski was in company with a wild man. He led me off into the woods where he'd jump off any bump he found. Noticing how often he fell and without breaking anything, I decided to try to imitate his actions. I fell more than 70 times that day (after lunch). Never broke or sprained anything. My friend taught me that I could ski without fear.

It is the *editing* wrung on the ladder that turns a mechanical project into something artful and engaging. Take it seriously and you'll breathe on a reader's soul.

CHAPTER EIGHT

NEVER LOOK BACK AND OTHER DISCIPLINES

Some of what you're about to read comes from "Stephen King on Writing."

It's his autobiography but contains several useful tips for wannabe writers. I don't read his novels, but this book is worth its weight in royalties.

He stomps on fear when he describes how he finished his first novel and then dumped it into the kitchen trash. He thought it was worthless.

His wife cajoled him until he sent it to a publisher. That book earned him $2 million.

Only You

King deals with fear in many practical ways. For me, the most important concept in the book is that your first draft is garbage, but *no one* will ever read it but you.

Think about that for a moment! The only person who will ever look at your first draft is you. Everyone else will see what you *edited* and it's the editing that refines trash into something worth reading.

Once I understood that one bit of truth, I bought Dragon and now hurry through those wretched first drafts with little emotional bleeding.

Never Look Back

A second bit of advice, from Stephen King, requires strong personal discipline: "Never look back!"

By this, he means that you should not even look at Chapter One while you *write* Chapter Three. Nor should you look at Chapter One while you *edit* Chapter Three. To look back is to turn yourself into a pillar of salt like Lot's wife in the Bible. She stopped to look at the disaster of Sodom only to smother in volcanic ash.

If you look back at the disaster, which lies behind, fear freezes your brain. The reason for this is quite simple, "What you wrote is not that good!" But you *can* massage trash into a worthy volume. What you write can't compare to your final edition.

Edit and Re-Edit

At two different times, in different places, I was privileged to meet authors whose books had impacted me many years earlier.

Both men told me the same thing. Their advice was to edit a manuscript at least 15 times before submitting it to a publisher.

Notice that I said, "at *least* 15 times." These guys were widely published and very good at their craft. Yet they held themselves to *discipline* that many would call overdone. I've done my best to imitate them. I'll go over this book 15 times before you ever lay eyes on it.

Each time I edit, I go through the book from page one to the end.

The first few passes are pretty painful. Around the fifth trip through the book, I'll print it on paper. A paper edit always shows up mistakes in grammar that I've overlooked on the laptop.

One important thing to look for as you edit the manuscript is any grammatically correct mistake. Twice, in this book, I've discovered the word "has," where I intended to say, "as." The weird thing is that in both instances the grammar was correct though the mistaken word generated a wrong meaning for the sentence.

The paper edit also shows up redundancies or structural flaws. I sometimes move chapters around at this point.

I hate messing with structure outside of the outlining process but sometimes the printed version shows me that I misplaced a concept, or an entire chapter. Don't know why the printout works so well, but as long as it does, I'll keep it up.

As the edits mount up the activity grows easier. By the time I get to the final pass through the book, I may change only four or five words.

The last few edits generate pleasure. By that time, I often awake in the middle of the night thinking of a word or phrase that might fit the book better than what I've already written. At this point, writing gets fun!

Discipline Yourself—Set Goals

King says you should view writing as work, *not* art.

He even advises a writer to move your desk way from that beautiful mountain view. Place it in a corner where you're not so easily distracted.

He also suggests that you set goals for yourself. In his case, he shoots for 10 pages per morning then takes the rest of the day off. If I were as successful as he is, I would probably do the same.

In my case I set aside blocks of time attached to milestones in my writing.

I collected notes for this book for several months. Numerous conversations with people, who have a book in them, motivated me to write this. They also filled my ToodleDo note-pad with dozens of ideas.

The outlining "event" would be a trip to another country. Knowing I would be in the air, or in airports, for 42 hours would afford the time to generate a rough outline. That was my goal. I would outline the book on that trip. I achieved more than the goal as I also wrote the rough draft of the first three chapters.

A few weeks later I faced a long morning with no interruptions. I set it aside to dictate the rest of this manuscript. In a couple of days, I travel again and will have evenings on my hands to edit the book the first few times. After that, I'll do what I explain in the following chapter.

My point here is that I set goals. I don't always achieve them but the simple act of setting them gets me on my way. Remember the cliché, "A journey of 1000 miles begins with the first step." Setting goals is step one.

Write A Long Letter

The best-selling book I ever wrote is called, "Starting A New Church." Regal published it nearly two decades ago, and it still sells well.

What might interest you is that I wrote it as a long letter to a friend.

My buddy, Mike Kai, had just assumed the pastorate of a church. The congregation was so small that it was much like starting from scratch.

One day over coffee he asked a bunch of questions about startup operations, momentum and other assorted "pastor things." I had already outlined the book, but Mike personalized it for me. I pictured him as I wrote. My goal was to answer his questions and meet the needs of his congregation. He gave me a new tool that day.

From that time till present I always picture an individual who I think would benefit from my writing.

I try to simply write a long letter to that person, structuring it as a book. Sometimes, I've found it helpful to tape a photo of a friend to the wall above my desk. Writing to a friend makes it more personal and causes me to be more open about personal feelings and experiences.

Bet you'd like to know if your picture is hanging on my wall…

CHAPTER NINE

WISDOM OF FIVE RED PENS

I've got a problem and so do you. You *can't* judge your own work fairly.

You need *objective input* at some point in the process because you're either too judgmental or too tolerant.

You can beat yourself to death with a pencil because your work is so poor. Or, you might inflate your head like a party balloon, believing that you'll make the New York Times bestseller list.

After editing my material 10 times, I ask for help. This usually comes in the form of five *volunteer* manuscript readers. Statistically, a higher percentage of women read books than men, so I usually ask three women and two men for their help.

Logic and Grammar

I ask my friends to look for *breaks* in my logic. The question I put to them is to be aware of wherever my logic looks like "A-B-D," instead of "A-B-C-D."

Appraising logic is the most vital gift they can offer. It's so easy to leave out part of a story because you know it too well. You assume that the reader knows the story as well as you do—bad mistake. It's as if a comedian told a joke but left out the segment leading into the punch line.

Another benefit from having friends look at your work is that they will correct your grammar. But you need to be careful here. You don't want to enlist an *amateur* English teacher (Maybe you should even avoid the real ones). They will pulverize your personal style, safeguarding proper grammar at the *expense* of colorful writing.

If I ask five people to read my work, at least one of them ignores what I said about logic and offers grammatical corrections instead. I pay attention to their work but try not to let them distort *my style* as an author. Besides, Microsoft mostly keeps my grammar in good shape with their grammar checking utility.

One caveat here is that Dragon Naturally Speaking can slip mistakes into your work from time to time. The software may misunderstand how you pronounce a certain word. This becomes a problem if it inserts a properly spelled, grammatically correct term that confuses your reader because it isn't what you meant to say. The "has" versus "as" illustration in the last chapter may have been a product of Dragon misunderstanding my pronunciation.

My "grammatical friends" always seem to catch one or two of these that I've missed. Just be careful that they don't wash the color out of your tapestry.

It's a good idea to insert page numbers into your manuscript before handing it to friends. Stapling pages together is also a good idea. You'll want to *remove* the page numbers before working with Amazon templates because they number your pages for you. Any pagination you add would seriously gum up the template.

Numbering is crucial, when you distribute your work among readers. This is because you'll need to interleave the (numbered) pages to link one friend's work to another for future edits. The compiled volume of your friend's work leads you through the next edit.

Five Red Pens

Along with the manuscript, you might find it practical to include five red pens.

The red pens make it easier for you to see the corrections while you edit. They also serve another function.

Inevitably, one of your friends will view your manuscript as something sacred. They'll present you with a well-critiqued manuscript complete with comments—which you can hardly read. This happens when a too respectful friend writes *very lightly* with a lead pencil. The manuscript is meant for marking. The red pens help that happen in a manner useful to you.

Three Is Enough

I always ask five people to help but sometimes get only three manuscripts in return. I've found that three *well-marked* versions of my book are enough to help me on my way. However, if I get five back, I always use them.

Stack the pages in order working from the back page of the book to the front. Include a single copy of any unmarked pages along with all the pages with significant red marks. The unmarked pages may not inform you of changes to make, but they will keep the manuscript readable, so it makes sense as you work your way through it.

You now progress through the book, editing according to the suggestions of your friends. This becomes your eleventh time to edit the book.

After that, let the manuscript *incubate* for a couple of weeks before running through it the final four times. The incubation period is not a time for total inactivity. You may find yourself driving on the freeway when a new thought or story pops into your brain. Go ahead and insert those ideas into the nearly finished manuscript. Those ideas enliven your nearly finished book.

When a couple of weeks pass, you can return to editing at a pretty rapid pace. By rapid pace, I mean back-to-back editing.

I'm not talking about rapid editing. The speed comes through one pass-through immediately following another. You keep moving but while intentionally working slowly.

The trick here is to *force* yourself to read slowly. There is a tendency to skim-read during the last few passes through the book. If you skim the book you will be sorry. You're bound to miss tiny but important details. The point of editing is to change *everything* that needs changing. That only happens if you take time to look for the small stuff.

As I said before, you won't make many changes during these last few runs. However, the changes you do make are the finishing touches that turn decent prose into art. Make them count!

SECTION 3:

Selling the Book

CHAPTER TEN

SELL THE SIZZLE…

This chapter appears in the wrong place in this book...on purpose!

I put it here because I imagine you would only begin thinking about these things *after* fully dreaming up your masterpiece.

You need to work on the elements in this chapter *concurrent* with the writing task. I only put them here because I assume you'd most naturally think about the process of writing before you got to marketing ideas.

You really do "sell the sizzle, not the steak" whenever someone buys your book.

Remember, there are dozens of people writing about the same subject. Ask yourself, "Why should anyone want to buy my book instead of others?" The answer to that question is why marketing is so crucial.

Think Like Steve Jobs

Think of this as Apple selling gorgeous *style* when someone is actually purchasing *technology*. The company creates value by making a phone or computer look and *feel* like Leonardo da Vinci heads their design team.

Ask yourself, "How can I make people *feel a compulsion* toward the information in my book?" The emphasis here is on that word "feel."

What is there about your book that might appear *compelling* to potential readers? You want people to believe that they cannot live without which you've written.

Focus, Focus, Focus

When I write for a mainstream publisher like Regal or Baker, they ask for a formal book proposal before they will even look at a manuscript. One section of the proposal is a three-part exercise designed to help an author bring focus to a project. The exercise is simple, yet painful: A. Describe the book in 250 words or less. B. Describe the book in 100 words or less. C. Describe the book in 30 words or less.

Cramming my bright ideas into 250 words compares to jamming my body into a tiny seat on a discount airline. It's hard!

After that it gets easier. Shrinking 250 into 100 and then 30 words isn't all that difficult. The reason? Regal has already helped me bring my thoughts into focus so *tightening* that focus is relatively easy.

Appealing Benefits

After cranking down the focus Regal asks a potential author to describe the *benefits* the reader will derive from the book. If I buy your book, what changes will it make in my life? Will it make life easier? Will my family benefit? Will I better my financial situation? What are you offering me that I value? This is where sizzle outsells steak at a barbeque.

Features That Deliver

Finally, Regal asks for a list of *specific features* which provide those benefits. What tools do you possess that will help the reader achieve the benefits you promised? How do your tools differ from whatever someone else might offer in their book?

Think of this entire chapter in terms of a book proposal. Be sure to include the elements I borrowed from Regal as you do.

The difficulty you face, if you publish with Amazon, is that you are the only person who will read the *completed* book before it is available to the whole world. This means that you need to think with a clear eye and a critical mind. Write a book proposal to yourself immediately *after* you construct your outline, but *before* you begin your first draft. Use the tools described in the previous paragraphs.

Keep your "book proposal" in printed form near you while writing. Refer to it often in order to maintain unity and focus as you write.

Three Devices for Selling Your Book

Convincing someone that they *need* your book first requires that you grab their attention. After that, you need to give them *solid reasons* for making the purchase.

Some of the following applies to print books that you might sell directly at a conference or some other such venue. All of it applies to potential buyers on Amazon whether they buy paperback books or download to Kindle. Remember, with Amazon you have just a couple of minutes to convince the buyer of the value of your product.

1. Choose A Title That Grabs Attention

A good place to begin looking for a title is in the book proposal, which I described, above. The 30-word description is probably the best tool for this.

Compile a list of all the *verbs*, which you used in that description. Then write a list of every *noun*. Randomly create combinations of verbs and nouns looking for something that grabs your attention.

Now type some of your word combinations into the Amazon search engine to look for the titles of other books addressing the same issues as yours. You don't want to copy but it's not a bad idea to glean ideas from the competition.

Though I don't use them, some of the best book titles involve alliteration. This tool doesn't work well for me but generates amazing results to other people.

I might have titled this book using words that begin with the letter "A." I could have called it "Amazing Authoring with Amazon" …but I didn't. You might notice that my brain isn't wired for alliteration. If yours is, take advantage of the opportunities available to you.

Remember, people don't read titles as much as they *scan* them.

It's best to grab the reader's attention with a two- or three-word title. You can always follow a short title with a longer, more descriptive subtitle.

The title should be pithy and drive a nail into the heart of what you have to say. Ask yourself what needs addressing and how you can force your ideas into just a couple of words. Focus, focus, focus!

2. Create A Lively Cover Design

Before you even think about designing a cover, go to Amazon.com and look at the covers as they appear on the page.

Did you notice that a book cover on Amazon is about the size of a large postage stamp? The problem is even worse if the buyer is working from a smart phone. Your cover *must be* simple and deliver a message in less than a second.

Don't attempt subtlety with either your title or your cover. Words must stand out and any photograph or illustration must *directly* speak to the purpose of the book.

Again, think about postage stamps as you design a cover. Granted, if someone finds your book by searching for it, they will see a somewhat larger image. But if they see it displayed in any other fashion on Amazon, or through social media, it will appear even smaller than a postage stamp.

Cover design can make or break your book. We'll spend more time on actual design in a later chapter. The two big lessons here are simplicity and eye-appeal.

A catchy cover is important enough that you might want to hire someone to design one for you. However, that can be a problem if you are an untested author. You don't want to spend more money on cover design then you make on the book.

Amazon has wonderful online tools to help you generate a good cover. We'll get to them when we look at formatting the book later on.

3. Write A Must-Read Book Description

After your title and cover, your Amazon book description is the most powerful tool for getting people to consider buying any book.

It would be easy to skip over the book description as a kind of necessary evil. Don't make that mistake. The book description should take several hours and much careful thought before you're done with it. Write and rewrite the description until you know that it delivers the goods.

Take a look at the competition. Note the good and the bad in other people's book descriptions. You'll notice that lots of people out there didn't read this book (or at least *this chapter*). Note the ineffectiveness of shorter descriptions and the usefulness of the longer ones. Grab ideas that work.

Extensive descriptions are best. Take advantage of *all the space* Amazon gives you to interface with a potential reader.

When writing the description, you should answer the following questions:

- What problem do you intend to solve?
- What tools do you offer to solve this problem?
- Does your book help alleviate pain?
- What will the reader lose if they don't solve their problem?
- What will the reader miss if they don't buy your book?
- What do you plan to teach that the reader doesn't already know (especially if they've read other books on the subject?
- How are you qualified to write this particular book?
- Does your book description appeal to the *emotions* of the potential buyer? Remember these are human beings looking for helpful answers.
- Did you write your description as though you're speaking to another person, face-to-face?
- Did you remember to include keywords that will help someone find you via a search engine? We'll address keywords in a future chapter.

There are other factors, which involve a buyer's decision-making process, but these are the big ones.

Make each of the above count and you stand a good chance with a potential buyer. Get sloppy with these and all the rest of your labor was in vain.

CHAPTER ELEVEN

Four Tools to Help Display Your Credentials

If you are an unknown author, you have a credibility problem.

The people in your own circle of influence will probably buy your book. But, what about the rest of the world? You need to convince others that your thoughts are valid.

The big question, which you must answer is, "What gives me the authority to write this book?"

Credibility counts and you must advertise it. Just because you wrote something doesn't mean that anyone will believe that you are an authority on your chosen subject.

You have a lot to say and probably have ample credentials to support your opinions. However, if the reader is unaware of those credentials they will simply move on to another author. It's up to you to *sell yourself* before you sell the material, which you have written.

Think about this. You're probably reading this book in an attempt to gather courage to write your first book. I'm assuming that you began trusting me *before* you make the purpose. You believed that I had the goods to help you achieve your goal or you wouldn't have risked your money.

Somehow, I sold myself to you before you bought my book. I did it by establishing my authority to write on the subject. I demonstrated credibility.

Overcome any sense of false humility and proclaim your worth with boldness.

You may know a great deal about your subject matter. You may have experiences, which directly speak to the reader's potential problems. However, if you don't convince the potential reader that you know your stuff there is no real reason for them to purchase your book.

Fortunately, there are several tools, which you can use to display your credibility to potential readers.

As you might expect, Amazon provides some of these tools. We discussed them before but not from the angle of establishing personal credibility. I hope to do that here.

1. Amazon Author's Page

The Amazon author's page is a core location to display your stuff. Please don't fall prey to the thought that this important device is simply an extra bit of Amazonian homework.

Their goal is to give you the opportunity to *engage* a potential reader. Your author page should give a short bio, some personal information to endear you to the reader. More important, it should communicate the *reservoir of knowledge,* which you draw from.

Was there a life-defining moment in your past? Describe it, if it has bearing on the subject matter of your book.

Be concise. This is not the place for hyperbole. Don't brag but do present yourself as an expert on your chosen subject. Be aware that your personal experiences make you something of an *expert* on any subject that has changed your life.

Look for differentiating factors that set you apart from the competition. Ask yourself, "What do I have to say that others don't?"

Have you written for other publishers? If so, then list the books, including a link to them on Amazon. How does your job or educational background qualify you? Do you train audiences outside of your primary position? Mention this as well, including the names of any groups, which would significantly add to your credibility.

2. Your Personal Website

As an author, you probably find yourself attached to a website hosted by someone else.

You may be an aspiring politician, a business leader or a pastor seeking to address a wider audience. In any case, if you show up on some organizational website include a link to that site in your Amazon author page.

You should *also* create a website of your own. This can be quite simple. You are shooting for web presence, not a complicated website. Its very existence contributes to your credibility as an author.

Include photos of yourself, a short bio and display your book along with any other books you have written. You may also want to offer free resources such as links to your YouTube videos or, perhaps, short papers that you offer as free downloads.

You can find my website at www.ralphmoorehawaii.com. I built it from an easy-to-use template that comes with my Go Daddy account. I spend less than four dollars a month for it.

You'll find swarms of offers for free websites if you just do a Google search.

As you might expect the free site is a teaser to get you to spend a few bucks. Go ahead and spend a little money to establish a presence on the internet.

Don't go overboard and spend a ton of money as all you really need is a basic presence. My website limits me to five pages before the price goes up. However, as of this writing I'm only using three of them.

Keep the design clean, simple and focused on your writing, or speaking if you are a public speaker.

When looking at web templates be advised that some, like WordPress, require a fair amount of expertise. Keep searching and you'll find companies offering their own very simple tools. GoDaddy is a great example of a one-stop shop.

3. Amazon Book Reviews

Credible reviews by previous readers move books. I believe that they are the *most powerful* weapon in your arsenal, aside from the Amazon Book Description.

I've noticed that the books, which I published through Regal began moving *only* after several people reviewed them online.

Consequently, I performed a test. I waited until one paperback/e-book gleaned a few reviews before mentioning it through social media. The book began selling immediately. I posted another book via social media *before* it obtained any reviews—there were almost *no sales* for a month.

After this test, I learned to solicit reviews from trusted and thoughtful friends.

I email credible individuals an offer for a free manuscript of my book if they are willing to review it on Amazon. About 60 percent of the people whom I ask, accept the offer.

I request that they review the book with *honesty*. I invite criticism as well as praise. Their negative comments help refine my writing skills and they lend credibility to the reviews. No book is perfect so the reviews should reflect that reality. In other words, you probably don't want your mom reviewing your book.

As soon as I've gathered six or seven reviews, I move ahead and let people know that the book is online. I do this through direct emails and via social media. This is a "kick-start" process and it works well.

4. The First 10 Percent of Your Book

Whether writing paperback or e-books for Kindle, you have the opportunity to give away a sample of your work. The sample displays your expertise, or lack of it. It also helps the reader know if they will enjoy your writing style.

With a paperback book, people can choose any part of the book, which they want to sample. However, most will look at the Table of Contents along with the first few pages of your work. A few, more careful, buyers may scan other parts of the book, but most will stick with the early pages. For that reason, this discussion, though it focuses on e-books, applies to print books as well.

You need to frontload your book with *value* for your readers.

Don't Waste Words

Don't waste space on words, which your prospective reader wouldn't appreciate.

This means that you *shouldn't* include information like a dedication, a forward, a list of your previous books or Library of Congress data.

You needn't worry about including endorsements either, since the reader will have already found them in the form of book reviews at the bottom of the Amazon sell page. All of that information may be quite meaningful to you, and you find it in most print books, but it works against you when working with both paperback and e-books. Make that first 10 percent count.

Focus your energies on a lively introduction, a descriptive table of contents and an engaging first chapter.

Write an Effective Introduction

The Introduction should pretty much reflect what you included in the Book Description posted on Amazon. A little *repetition* helps reinforce your offer of value in exchange for time and money the reader will invest in the book.

Ensure that your Introduction is strong and presents value to the reader. If your book contains a list of specific helps, then describe that list in the introduction.

While you're at it, let's *not* call this section "Introduction." Let's use these words, "Why You Should Read This Book." A little boldness works wonders when you attempt to motivate others.

Keep Your Table of Contents Interesting

Invest time developing *lively* chapter titles. They are strong selling points. Dull chapter titles suggest a dull book. Work hard to develop titles, which pique your reader's attention.

Does your Table of Contents *shout* at a reader with *action* verbs? Does it accurately describe the benefits packed into each chapter? Does it appeal to a reader's sense of adventure or fun?

I finalize my own Amazon purchase decisions based on the Table of Contents. After sorting through the title, cover, book description and reviews everything hinges on that short list of chapter headings. If the chapters look interesting, I hit the "Add to Cart" button. If the chapters appear boring, I move on to the competition. Make your Table of Contents dance.

Give Chapter One Your Best Attention

Give a lot of thought (and extra editing) to "Chapter One," because it may be the only part of the text a reader ever sees. They won't read the rest of the book unless the first chapter works for them. Remember, Amazon works hard to distribute your first chapter as a "free sample" of the rest of the book. Make it count!

In a perfect world, every chapter would be wonderful. That may work for you. It doesn't work for me.

I beat my brains out trying to write the best book possible. At some point, mental fatigue sets in and all the chapters run together in my head. When that happens, I know I've stretched my brain about as far as possible. I have little mental energy left for that particular volume. At that point the book is pretty well finished…all but the first chapter.

After completing a book, I let the manuscript sit for a few extra days then go back over the first chapter several more times. Chapter One *must* pop!

You must insure that people find *wonder* in your first chapter. If they don't, they'll simply move on to another author.

In this chapter, we've looked at four powerful sales tools. Did you notice that Amazon provides all but one, your personal website? They are capable of helping you market your material in ways which no conventional publisher could even approach. How you use the tools is up to you.

CHAPTER TWELVE

HELP PEOPLE FIND YOUR BOOK

There are several ways for a reader to find your book.

The first two are a product of chance mixed with your ability to promote your work via email and social media. The others encompass a working relationship between you and Amazon.

Each of these methods offers its own unique benefits. Some are more costly for you than others. For instance, writing a blog is time-consuming and may not bring the results you anticipate.

My own postings through various social media generate great benefits. I list my books, among other things, on Pinterest. I regularly mention, and link to them, through short blurbs on Face-book and Twitter. Social media pays off, particularly if *other people* mention my books in their postings. We'll talk more about that in the next chapter.

Paid advertising through social media or even through Google has proven that it doesn't provide much of an *immediate* return for me. Both Face-book and Google ads *do* help kick-start sales although they do not generate enough income to directly pay for themselves. However, I believe that increased momentum generated by ads usually pays off in the *longer term*. I use ads, but as a small volume author, I continue to use them sparingly. I'm always very aware of cost versus effectiveness when spending any money on my writing projects.

If I pay for ads, I normally choose Face-book over Google because Face-book only advertises to people who are linked to me as friends or followers whereas Google markets to the general public.

Face-book pre-prices the ads according to content while Google charges according to keywords. With Google, you can set a maximum price that you are willing to pay per click. Start with a dime a click and work up from there. The cheaper keywords generate the most clicks; therefore, they present a better use of funds. You wouldn't want to pay extra for someone to find your book through a keyword that didn't really relate to the content of your book.

I only run one or two ads immediately after a book release. The goal is to juice momentum while the book is still new. After that, the value of ads rapidly diminishes.

Let's talk about ways in which an active searcher can find your product at no cost to you. By, "Active searcher," I mean a person with a *felt need* who is searching for answers, which you may offer in you book.

1. Searching by Your Name

If someone knows you, they probably know about your book, or at least about the experiences, which may have led to the book. This could result in an Amazon search by your name. This is probably the *weakest* sales tool available to you. Though it is valuable, it really doesn't help Amazon market your book. You are on your own with this tool.

2. Searching Book Title

Here again, only those with inside knowledge will be able to find your book. The tool works, however, it's not all that useful.

I previously mentioned the two powerful tools, which do generate "search by title" results. These are personal emails and announcements via social media. Use them boldly!

I usually send emails to everyone in my contact list that might benefit from a new book. I know people hate spam, but your friends like you. Because they like you, they are probably interested in your project based on the strength of your friendship. The email should include a small picture of the front cover along with a link to the book on Amazon.

When using social media *repetition* is important. I start by mentioning that I am writing the book a few weeks before I intend to release it. Later I "express relief" that it is about to be published (Yes, this is advertising, but there is truth in it—I post my relief because it is a real part of my life on that day). Finally, I announce the release (after posting the book and reassuring myself that there are book reviews in place.

After the book is available and selling, I'll announce its presence a couple of times in succession. Then I report on its growing sales (don't mention specific numbers, just the fact that it is moving). You may want to report on your book as it climbs the sales ranking figures which Amazon publishes for every book, every day.

Finally, I repeat what others say about my books. Often when someone writes something nice about the book, as a review or a personal message, I re-post their words (protecting their identity in the post). Each time I post something about the book, I include a link to the Amazon page where potential readers can find the book.

3. Keyword Search

The "Keyword Search" is where we begin to *strike gold* with Amazon.

Take, for example, my book "Defeating Anxiety." Quite obviously, anyone searching under the keyword, "anxiety," might chance upon the book.

However, there are any keywords associated with the pain felt by an anxious person. You might think of words like stress, depression, fear or host of others. These terms could help a person discover my book.

Just how do you go about tying effective keywords to your book? How do you make it easier for a person with a problem to discover your solution?

A Little Help from Google

I already mentioned Google AdWords as an avenue to boost momentum when you release your book. AdWords also offers itself as a prime tool for discovering and developing effective keywords.

You begin by typing, "Keyword Planner," into your Google browser. You should see a page pop-up, which asks you to create an account with Google AdWords.

Go ahead and create the account, understanding that you need not advertise with Google in order to use the tools. In fact, you don't even have to give them credit card information unless you actually create and activate an advertisement.

Once you've established your account, sign in. A page then opens to guide you through the process of creating and activating an advertisement. However, at this point, your interest is only in "Keywords," so click the link which says, "Tools and Analysis" at the top of the page. Under that link you will find the words, "Keyword Planner." Click this link to access the tool.

The Keyword Planner

Once you open the Keyword Planner, click on "Search for new keyword and ad group ideas." A box will open, offering four options. You want to utilize the first one, which is titled, "Your product or service." Now list several keywords, which you associate with your book (Glean these from your trusty book proposal). Then click the "Get Ideas" button at the bottom of the page.

After clicking, "Get Ideas," a new page will appear. It has two tabs at the top, one is labeled, "Ad group ideas," the other is, "Keyword ideas." Click on, "Keyword ideas." When you do, you'll find more keywords that he could possibly use.

For, "Defeating Anxiety," I entered, "anxiety, stress, fear, and depression." The result was more than 800 suggestions from Google. Now the trick is to narrow down the range of keywords.

At this point, you double-click the top of the column called "Competition," under "Keyword (by relevance)." Look at the high-competition keywords and select 15-20 which most appeal to you. The high-competition words are those terms directly matching your book to potential searchers.

It may feel counterintuitive to look for high competition words. They only become high competition because they appear most often in Google searches. These are the words in the minds of the most people. Low competition, on the other hand, indicates low interest.

Back to Amazon

Now switch to Amazon.

Begin to create combinations of the keywords, which you found on Google; testing them via Amazon's search engine.

Look for words that bring up lots of results because that indicates interest—these are Amazon's version of high competition keywords. You might even try combinations of keywords or put the words "How to…" in front of your keywords. Another trick is to add the word "book" to your keyword.

Again, are looking for words that show lots of results. The goal is for lots of people to discover your work through random online searches.

Amazon will ask you to list keywords as part of the publishing process. They attach *hidden* keywords to your work. But, the value of keywords doesn't stop there. It's wise to use your best three or four keywords *several times* in your book description, introduction and first chapter. All three areas show up in the search engines.

4. Category Search

Amazon allows you to list your book under two categories. The category list is theirs so you can't make up categories of your own.

You may want to start by looking at the competition. You'll find category information at the very bottom of an Amazon page depicting any book. The heading reads, "Look for Similar Items by Category." It goes on to show you the two categories pertaining to whatever book you have selected.

Learn from your competitors but do not be afraid to branch out on your own. The idea here is to *test* a category for a couple of weeks then test another. This involves a lot of guesswork and intuition.

It's especially important when your book is not selling in one category to give it a shot in another. Whatever you do, plan to benefit from the established competition. Competitors' books selling well in a given category should tell you something about where to lodge your own work.

CHAPTER THIRTEEN

GATHER SUPPORT FROM YOUR READERS

People used to say, "The best advertising is by word-of-mouth."

Today that may no longer be true.

The best advertising may be a recommendation via social media. There are three ways to solicit this from others.

"Before You Go"

This first tool applies *only* to Kindle e-books. Amazon created a feature, which appears on the last page of every Kindle e-book. A page pops up with the heading,

"Before You Go." It then asks the reader to rate the book, giving it between one and five stars. It also leaves space for the reader to write a few words about the book.

If the reader has linked their Kindle account to any social media outlet, their estimation of your book appears for all their friends to see. A few kind words can go a long way towards helping others discover that your book potentially meets their needs.

This is a powerful tool, which you should *never* overlook. The problem many authors have is that they include material after the final page of their actual book. Doing so places the *Before You Go* option after that extra material.

There are sometimes good reasons for doing this but if you do you better be convinced it is worth the possibility that a reader may never see the Before You Go page.

Be careful not to waste this opportunity with data, which might not be interesting to your readers. If you load up the back end of the book with non-essentials (the kind of dedications, etc. that writers often include in the front of their book) you won't get those precious recommendations from your readers.

In some cases, I have chosen to insert a free chapter from another book at the end of my book *before* the reader comes to the Before You Go function.

I've only included free chapters in books, which offer the opportunity to cross-sell each other. In this situation, I believe the free sample carries a higher priority than the Before You Go option. The sample chapter doesn't replace the other option, but it does put a barrier between it and the last sentence of the current book.

Cross-selling grows more effective as you generate more titles. This is especially true if your books form a series or relate to each other in terms of subject matter. Remember, if you have a long book it could become a series of three or four shorter books. People like books in series and today's readers like short books.

A Personal Plea for Help

Just before the end of a book, I ask the readers to interact with me and to help me promote the book.

This part of the book needs to establish *personal* contact between you, as author, and your readers. You need their help and they need to understand how important their help can be to you as well as to others.

I usually end my manuscript with a header, which says, "In Conclusion." Under this heading, I thank the readers for investing time in my book. I offer personal access through both my Face-book page and my webpage. I invite them to contact me with any questions or suggestions about what I've written.

After this, I tell them what a great *favor* it would be to me if they would mention my book through their own media outlets. I also ask them to rate the book in with the Before You Go feature.

Of course, what I've just written gets modified in a print book sold through Kindle. With print books there is no opportunity to quickly rate the book online, so I just include the plea for help, which I've outlined here.

Don't be shy about asking for help. People like to do nice things for those who have helped them. If your book is useful then you can expect readers to help other people find it.

Remember also that a direct request will move people to action when they might not have done so otherwise. Be bold!

Interfacing with Readers

When someone does take time to write me about my work, I always write back. Failure to do so would be rude.

If they write about the book and how it helped them, I thank them for their kindness and ask them, again, for a personal favor. That favor is, "Because the book helped you, I would consider it a great personal favor if you would mention it to your friends through social media." Many do.

Depending on what the reader has said, I may quote them on my own Face-book and Twitter profiles. I change key details to protect the identity of the writer, but I assume their stories will help others, so I pass them on.

Occasionally someone sends a Face-book message that I would rather not read. Either they found that the book fell short of their expectations or, perhaps, they simply disagree with something I wrote. I always look at these contacts as opportunities.

If you treat a critic with respect you may well win a new friend. I know of at least one situation where a critical reader made a big deal of telling others that I had responded positively to their criticism. Their first words hurt. Their later words helped other people gain interest in the book as a useful tool. They probably helped people *discover* me as an author.

While we're discussing criticism let's talk for a moment about negative comments left on the Amazon page where readers can rate your book.

My advice: "Simply ignore them." Do not attempt to contact or in any way react to criticism in public. You can only make yourself look bad. If someone gets abusive report them, but short of that silence is the best tactic.

CHAPTER FOURTEEN

FORMATTING WITH TEMPLATES

This chapter appears at the end because formatting is the last task you face.

Formatting for Amazon can be both easy and difficult at the same time.

It's easy because Amazon wants you to use only the simplest commands in your word processor, and because they provide straightforward templates to turn your document into a book.

Two Templates and A Convertor

Amazon provides two templates for paperback books. The first generates the interior of your project, while the second allows you to design your own cover. Finally, they offer you the ability to convert your paperback book into e-book format.

The Amazon templates for the inside of the book are in Microsoft Word format, so it is best if you generate your manuscript in Word before downloading the templates.

As an alternative, Amazon does give you directions for creating a pdf of your manuscript using other software. This, however, would require paying someone with the proper expertise to do the job—not a smart expenditure for an untried author.

The templates are quite simple, but you'll invariably make mistakes on your first go-around. I still make occasional errors even though I've used the templates several times. But, working with Amazon's templates is much like riding a bicycle—once you get the hang of it, you can almost do it with your eyes closed.

You build the book, download an approximation of the finished product, then correct the mistakes you find. It takes a little time. You just need patience to fully understand the tools.

Kindle begins by asking information about the project such as the title, any author who partnered with you, etc.

After gathering the necessary info, they issue an ISBN number for the sake of libraries or bookstores.

At this point they offer you the opportunity to download one of their *interior* templates. They come in a variety of sizes ranging from 5x8 inches up to 6x9. Shorter books look best if you choose one of the smaller formats. I like 5x8 for paper books, though my (longer) Baker books are all 6x9. There are other sizes, but these are the ones which suite me best.

Word Stuff

While writing the book (long before you think about templates) there are four things to keep in mind.

Avoid excessive formatting

The "tricks" that you normally use in Word might not translate well into the Amazon templates.

Never use the Tab key to indent

Always set up your document using the Paragraph function in Word. Amazon templates easily understand paragraph formatting.

The "Change Case" function in Word causes problems

If you want to capitalize something, do it manually. The Change Case function in Word creates problems when you load your document into the templates. This is a small bother when you compare it to the ease the template brings into your life.

Never include page numbers, headers or footers

If your manuscript contains these page numbers, headers or footers; you'll run into trouble. Create Space tries to duplicate them. They add page numbers and headers automatically (You can, however, add page numbers before enlisting your five friends with the red pens. Just be sure to remove them before loading the manuscript into the template).

Kindle suggests that you use the "Styles" function in Word. Apparently, this simplifies everything. However, for some reason I am utterly confused by Styles, so I never bother with it.

Begin with Your Paperback Version

If you start with paper, or print on demand, you can easily morph your product into an e-book through Kindle. But if you begin with Kindle and then try to change it to paperback you are in for technical hitches. I know, that is how I went about creating "Defeating Anxiety." Wasted a lot of time on that one.

The reason for this is simple. Paperback cover-design templates easily adapt to e-books. Kindle offers no such option coming from the e-book side.

If you start with an e-book you also have to design your own matching paperback cover which would be very difficult unless you are good at Photoshop, which I am not.

As I write this chapter, I realize that it sounds a bit complicated, but you will grasp how easy it is once you jump into this part of the project.

The Inside of Your Book

When manipulating paper book formatting you simply follow directions step-by-step. The website directs you through the process.

ISBN Numbers

As I mentioned before, Amazon will provide an ISBN number before you get to the templates. Don't purchase your own ISBN or you will waste money.

One thing to note about ISBN numbers is that yours will evaporate if you ever take your book out of print. Lots of people criticize Amazon for this. The truth is that they recycle the numbers for out of print books. I don't see the rub.

If your book goes out of print, no bookstore will attempt to buy it anyway. Besides, books only go out of print once sales slow enough that publishers can no longer afford to store them. It is pretty difficult to imagine that happening when your book only occupies a few megabytes on a hard drive.

Amazon has every motive for keeping your project alive even if it sells very slowly. They make money on every single sale.

Fonts

Your primary responsibility will be to understand the template and to load your Word document into it. You need to consider fonts that work well together. Amazon templates come with preset fonts, but you can change them. There are websites, which compare fonts in combination with each other. These are free but be careful because *not all fonts* work well with Amazon.

Blank Pages

One thing to watch is that every *significant* page in the book appears as a *right-hand* page, rather than on the *left* as you hold the book open. This includes your title page, introduction, Chapter One etc.

I struggled with this several times before I realized that what appears on the template as I construct it is *not exactly* what appears as the finished product.

Fortunately, Amazon allows you to preview the finished product before publishing a proof copy as a final test. Whenever you think you've finished working with the template, Amazon processes it then spits it back to you as it should appear in printed form.

I found that even though the template showed blank pages on the left with significant pages on the right everything ran together with no breaks between chapters, etc. The solution was to manipulate the template so every section head or first page of a chapter appeared on the left-hand side of the template. It is counterintuitive but it is how it works—think about it: the first page of any book appears on the right, but it shows up on the left side of the template.

Create blank pages in Word via the "Page Layout" menu. Click on "Breaks," then click "Next Page."

When creating blank pages, be sure to delete the page number in the footer at the bottom of the page. The page will still be numbered, it just won't be viewable to a reader. Remove numbers, also, on any pages, which contain photos or graphics. Remember, you want your book to look as professional as it would if released by a big-name publishing company.

To delete headers and page numbers from a single page in Word, you first click on the header or footer space. Then click the button called "Link to Previous." This allows you to delete the header or page number without altering the rest of your headers and footers.

I *promise* that you will struggle with the template. However, when you're finished, you'll find yourself laughing at the simplicity of the mistakes you made. It might be a good idea to take notes during this phase to make it easier when you to your next book.

Seven Steps to An Effective Book Cover

Once you've completed the interior of the book, Amazon will approve it and then automatically move you to cover design.

These templates are very straightforward but there are a few pointers I need to give you:

1. Keep It Simple

Keep your cover very simple as it will be displayed at the size of a postage stamp when someone looks for it online.

2. *Seldom Reverse Type*

You should always use "dark-on-light" copy in your cover text. Reverse type gets less attention from a buyer.

I got that piece of advice from an executive at a large publishing company. He told me that graphic artists love "reverse type" (light copy against a dark background), but their extensive testing demonstrated that reverse print books don't sell as well as the conventional dark-on-light scenario.

3. *Picture People*

The cover design should include people *facing the camera* if possible. If they can't face the camera have them facing away, but *always* use people. Graphic designers are into cool, readers are into people.

An excellent place to buy photos is at Shutterstock.com. For about $20 you gain the commercial rights to some very beautiful photos. Better yet, there are thousands to choose from.

A side note here is that you can upload Shutterstock's massive photo files to the Kindle template with no problem. You don't even need to change the dpi settings though they are far higher than Kindle asks for. As long as you exceed the minimum, Kindle does the rest.

There are a host of companies selling photos, but I've found Shutterstock easiest to work with. You can buy in bulk. I gave them 49 dollars and get to choose five photos at my leisure.

One Shutterstock feature I really love is called a "Lightbox." After typing a keyword, you find yourself inundated with hundreds, even thousands of photos. You can move whatever attracts your interest to your Lightbox then sort out the best in a later session.

4. *Utilize Variety*

Paperback templates come in many different styles. But you'll want to modify them to fit your personality and the thrust of your book. Please notice that you can change fonts, change the colors of the fonts and change the background colors of the book. Play with this function and you come up with something that truly reflects the content of your project. Of course, the photos and written blurbs also personalize your book.

You'll be amazed at the incredible range of creativity available—all for free. There is no need to hire a graphic artist until you become a best-selling author.

5. Include A Spine

One thing worth mentioning here is the "spine" of the book. If the book is to thin there won't be room for your name, or the title, on the spine. There are several solutions to this.

You can use a smaller format for the overall size (5x8 inches is the smallest available). You may want to enlarge your fonts. And, be sure you leave blank left-hand pages after each chapter.

Play around with paragraph formatting. Instead of single-spacing use the multiple-space feature, in Word. I find that 1.15 spaced documents look appealing. I also like to include 6 pt. spacing between paragraphs. If this seems complicated, just open the "Paragraph" dialogue box in Word and experiment with it. You'll master it in 90 seconds.

One note of interest is that the paperback templates offer just 10 chapters. Most books go longer than this. Assuming that yours does, simply copy and paste chapter 10 several times at the end of the book. Be sure to label each chapter according to its new number. Then go to the Table of Contents and modify it accordingly.

6. *Order A Proof Copy*

When you're all done with your masterpiece, order a proof copy.

Proofs are cheap and can save you a boatload of grief. If you made undiscovered template errors, they will show up. I've even discovered a missing period at the end of a sentence. The proof is an easy step to want to skip, but it is necessary.

My last book looked perfect using the paperback Previewer. When I got the proof, I found that I had a "header" at the top of three blank pages. I simply went back and deleted it the template. Had I gone to print without seeing the proof I would've been embarrassed.

This book stymied me in that there were header/footer errors which I could not see in the Previewer. A phone call to Kindle drew a prompt and polite answer. Very helpful.

Moving on To the E-book

When you finish with your print book, a screen will offer to turn your print book into a Kindle e-book for a price. Don't spend the money.

After you reject the option, Amazon will immediately offer you the use of the front cover of your paperback book as the cover for your electronic edition, but at no cost to you.

Now it's time to load your Word document into the e-book template. Again, don't bother with headings or page numbers. This is particularly important since Kindle e-books appear on smart phones, computer screens and on Kindle reading devices. In every case the pagination is different. Amazon automates this process and anything you insert will confuse readers of e-books.

Another thing to remember is that you must delete any blank pages from your paperback book when you convert it to electronic. This is because Kindle doesn't involve right-hand or left-hand pages. A blank space in a Kindle e-book would only confuse your readers.

CHAPTER FIFTEEN

AN AUTHOR'S CHECKLIST FOR SUCCESS

By now your head may be spinning with details.

Writing my first book overwhelmed me. I felt as if I were in 8th grade trying to drag out that first 1,000-word term paper.

So, take a deep breath. Remember that each function outlined in this book is fairly simple of itself. Just live in the moment. Work on each step as an individual project and you'll be surprised at how easy it is to publish with Amazon.

Remember, it is no more difficult to write and publish with Amazon than with a conventional publisher (or even a vanity printer). The difference with Amazon is that they toss in all those extra tools to help you sell the book. Don't let the tools overwhelm you—master them!

This is a review chapter. It's actually a checklist designed to give you an overview of the process from beginning to end.

Getting Started

1. Begin jotting notes in your smartphone or a small notebook.
2. Print your notes, cut the printout into individual notes which you can lay in piles on the floor or a large table.
3. Build your outline from the piles you created. Don't stop with the notes, work the outline into a detailed roadmap so you always know what to write next.

Think About Marketing

4. Write your own book proposal. Summarize the book in 250, then 100 and finally 30 words.
5. Develop a working title. From the summary glean combinations of words which will help you invent a working title (Titles tend to change during the writing process).

6. Write a 650-700 word "Book Description" that you would like to appear on the Amazon page where they sell your book.

Generate the Manuscript

7. Begin the writing process by purchasing Dragon Naturally Speaking (Home Edition) from www.nuance.com. It currently sells for $59.00. You'll save that much in time when you write your first book.

8. Talk your outline into a first draft of the book. Remember it will be bad and there is little you can do about that. The important issue here is spitting out your ideas. You will refine them later.

Edit Your Manuscript into A Thing of Beauty

9. Edit ten times from beginning to end. Never look back while writing or editing. Do your fifth edit on paper to help you see the book in a different light. Let the manuscript "rest" a minimum of three days between these edits.

10. Give five copies of your manuscripts along with five red pens to friends who enjoy reading. (Be sure to add page numbers before you distribute the manuscripts—you can remove them before working with paperback templates.

11. Harvest your friend's ideas. Disassemble the five manuscripts then pull them together in one thick manuscript using only the pages, which they marked. Edit their thoughts into your working manuscript.

12. Edit five more times.

Design the Actual Book

13. Go to Kindle and begin the process of registering the book.

14. Download the correct template for your project. Load your manuscript into the template and massage it into a presentable book.

15. Open the cover generator. Insert photos and play with colors and styles till you are satisfied.

16. Order a proof-copy of your book. When it arrives, read it very *slowly*. Might be good advice to get a friend who is unfamiliar with the book to look at the proof copy (You can order several proofs and they are quite inexpensive).

17. Once you approve the proof copy move on to the Kindle template. Be sure you modify the end of the book as paper books do not offer the "Before You Go" option.

Price Carefully

18. Price the books as both paperback and electronic editions. Remember the rule of thumb about non-fiction Kindle e-books selling for $4.99 (as of this writing). I usually price my books at $9.99 in paper and $4.99 as Kindle e-books. This allows for easy sales if I take the book with me to a public speaking venue.

Promote the Book

19. Make sure your Amazon Author Page sells *you* as an author. Keep it friendly, not scholarly. People buy books from people they like. Mention your family, your hobbies and any other activity, which might endear you to others.
20. Solicit book reviews from credible people. Do this by first asking them if they would review your book if you give it to them for free. Be sure they don't honey coat the recommendations. You want credibility more than smooth words. Recommendations sell books more than any other factor.
21. Email your friends and jump on social media to let the world know about your book. If you are a public speaker, be sure to purchase a case or two to sell at events where you address others.

22. Be sure you choose Keywords and Categories which will help people find the book. You may want to change these after a couple of weeks just to find the "sweet spot."

23. Buy and read the competition. Then leave nice reviews on their Amazon pages—be sure to identify yourself as the author of your own book, here.

24. Track your sales daily. Determine if offering your book for free (start with just two days—Wednesday and Thursday) would help jump-start sales). Remember, the free book offer works best if you've written more than one.

25. Don't get discouraged. Your sales will ebb and flow. Look at your first book as an experiment. By the time you've finished the first one you probably have ideas for others. Have fun writing—at the very least it is a nice hobby. At your best, you will help change some lives.

26. Get to work…

In Conclusion

Before you go, I'd like to ask you a favor…If the book was helpful to you, I figure that you owe me just a little.

The purpose of this book is to help people who have a story crawl out of the prison of fear and get to writing. I had so many conversations with potential authors that I finally hung them on Amazon in the form of this book.

Because the people I most want to help are my personal friends I did little to promote the book other than email you or tell you about it over coffee.

I really believe you have something to say or I wouldn't have told you about what I've written here. So, here's the deal…

If this small book got your juices flowing, please do two things for me. They will cost you no money. What I need are your endorsements on Amazon and on social media.

If you're willing …

First, go back and write a short review on the Amazon page where you bought the book. When you do, please message me via Facebook since I may want to quote your words elsewhere.

Also, any mention via your own social media would help a lot. If you can include a link back to the Amazon page, it would help even more. Thank you in advance!

ABOUT RALPH MOORE

Ralph is the Founding Pastor of Hope Chapel Kaneohe Bay in Hawaii and of Hope Chapel in Hermosa Beach, California. He recently retired from his latest church plant, Hope Chapel Honolulu to join the team at Exponential.org where he serves as Church Multiplication Catalyzer.

Beginning with just 12 people, the Hope Chapel 'movement' has mushroomed to more than 2,300 churches worldwide. Ralph travels extensively teaching pastors in newly launched movements how to rapidly multiply churches.

Catch up with him at ralphmoore.net/ or google for "The Ralph Moore Podcast."

A partial list of Ralph's books includes:

- Let Go of The Ring: The Hope Chapel Story
- Defeating Anxiety
- Starting A New Church
- Making Disciples
- How to Multiply Your Church
- Mega/Multi/Multiply (Free at Exponential.org)
- New to Five (Free at Exponential.org)
- You Can Multiply Your Church (Free at Exponential.org)